What long ears you have!

Photograph by courtesy of the Sevenoaks Chronicle

arco pet handbooks

Donkeys

Robin Stothard

with a foreword by
SUSAN GREENWAY
Honorary Secretary
Donkey Breed Society

New York

Published 1973 by Arco Publishing Company, Inc.
219 Park Avenue South, New York, N.Y. 10003

Copyriyght © 1971 by G. Bell and Sons, Ltd.
Library of Congress Catalog Card Number 72-3335
ISBN 0-668-02665-0

Printed in the United States of America

Contents

Where have you been hiding?

DEDICATION

To Jackdaw my faithful and much loved hunter after whom our Stud is named.

ACKNOWLEDGEMENTS

My thanks to my great friend and Vet Tom van Laun who has patiently given so much of his valuable time to all our Donkey problems.

Also to Harold Bennett whose photographs have added so much to this book.

Finally to my family whose encouragement has been such a great help to me while writing this book.

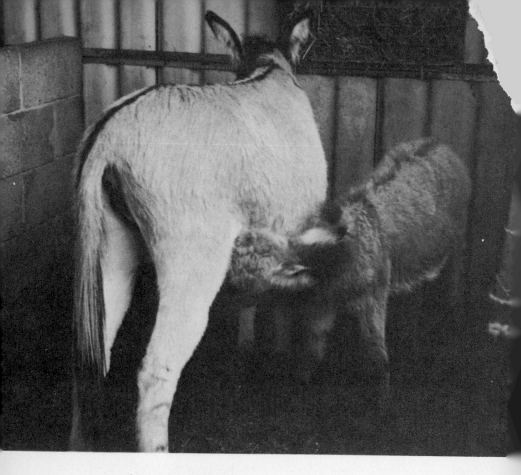

Back to the Milk Bar

Foreword

by SUSAN GREENWAY

Donkeys are an integral part of the lives of Robin Stothard and her husband, and when I visited them this summer, shortly after reading this book in manuscript, I was struck by the tranquility of the Jackdaw Donkey Stud. There appeared to be none of the usual bustle, and indeed, it seemed as if they do not so much run a Stud as allow their donkeys as natural an environment as possible in this country, around which they are constant and very welcome visitors.

This seemingly effortless management is misleading and the secret is to be found in this book and particularly in two comments Mrs. Stothard makes: the first, dealing with bad habits, "to gain your donkey's respect means that you have to achieve quite a high standard of behaviour yourself"; and the second, "the important thing about dealing with animals is to be ready and to anticipate just in case you need to be resourceful". You can hardly go wrong if you keep these two maxims in mind.

If a child is a member of a Pony Club, this book will underline much that he or she already knows about animal management, but for those with no previous experience of donkeys, and for their parents, it will be of immense value. It is just what it sets out to be – a Guide for beginners. There is also much in it of great value to the hardened devotee of the donkey.

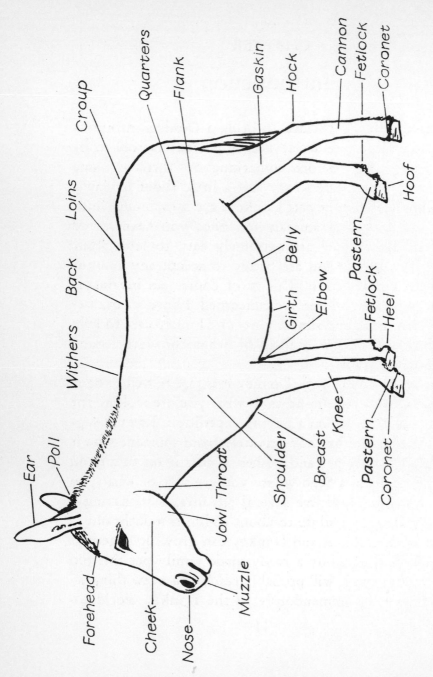

The Points of the Donkey

CHAPTER 1

Introduction

Having finally decided to bring a Donkey into your family circle there are several important factors to be considered, but before embarking on these at some length, I would like to say just a little about having a Donkey as a family pet. Donkeys are most undemanding and endearing animals and once you have sorted out a routine they are extremely easy to look after. They like people and are happy to accept any amount of love and affection. This is, of course, an invaluable quality where children are concerned. I have set out below some basic and simple hints on Donkey care to help beginners to know a little of what they are letting themselves in for.

When choosing your Donkey it is just as well to have some ideas in your mind as to what you are looking for before setting out on a buying expedition. I would suggest that you either buy privately from someone who is selling a family pet and wishes to pass it on to a good home, or from a Stud where you are sure of what you are getting. There are several advantages in having a young Donkey foal up to about eighteen months old as then both children and Donkey can grow up together. However if you buy a ready-made family pet this too can be fun and it will probably teach you a few things.

Prices vary tremendously in the Donkey world today, and I think it is safe to say that it simply depends on what you buy and where you buy it. A mare, filly or gelding will all make splendid family friends. I believe people favour a mare or filly simply because they feel that one day she may be able to have a little foal. I suggest that if you decide to buy a colt, unless you are going to use him later for stud purposes, it is wise to have him gelded. As a colt foal grows up, his natural male instincts make it most difficult to keep him as a pet. People with years of experience can still meet up with problems when keeping a stallion even though he may be used at stud. He can become both very strong and agressive, and it is neither kind nor practical to attempt to keep him as a bachelor. It is wise to check on age. No one ever seems to have a Donkey to sell which is over about fifteen, and this usually means that they have lost count of the years! Not that it is important to be aware of the fact that you are buying an antique, but all things being equal the younger your Donkey is when you first bring him into your family the more years of his life there should be to share with him. Height is measured at the withers and over 36ins high is measured in hands, (4ins to each hand). Miniatures are under 36ins, small standards are 36ins to 10½ hnds. Standards are 10½ hnds to 12 hnds and over 12 hnds are the very large Spanish Donkeys.

Colour is entirely up to the individual. There are many colours to choose from and all have the cross on their back except for the pure white Donkeys and broken coloured Donkeys. The latter are black and white, brown and white or tri-coloured.

CHAPTER 2

Accommodation

GRAZING. Firstly you must consider what facilities you have available for grazing. I recommend a paddock or orchard of not less than half an acre. However I do know of many cases where a Donkey is kept on a much smaller area and seems to be quite happy. The quality of the grass is not too important and Donkeys usually favour a rather coarse type of grass. It is wise to make sure that there is no ragwort in your field or yew in the hedge because these are very poisonous to Donkeys. It is also a good idea to see that there are no rabbit holes or pot holes or pieces of wire lying around.

It is important to see that your grass is not grazed too hard. If you only have a small paddock, try to divide it during the summer months so that the grass has time to freshen up. You can use an electric fence for this purpose. This is more economical than permanent fencing and can be moved about to different parts of the field as it is essential to have some sort of rotational grazing for your pasture to keep it worm free. Where pasture is poor and over grazed there is often a worm problem.

While dealing with the field it seems a good moment

13

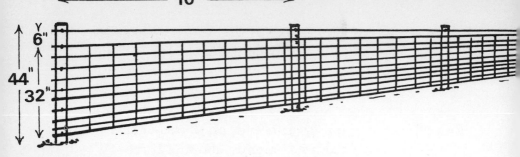

Posts — 5½ feet. Staples — 1¼ inches. Wire — C.832/12. Top wire — No. 8 gauge, stranded

to talk about the fencing problem. In the first place Donkeys are extremely curious animals and the other side of the fence seems to have a fatal fascination for them, even though they are quite content on their own home ground. For this reason it is wise to see that all fences are Donkey-proof as far as possible. We find that 32" high pig netting C.832/12 which is usually in 55yard rolls, with a single strand of 8 gauge stranded wire stapled about 6" above to 5½ft fencing posts at 10ft intervals is most satisfactory. It is both dangerous and unnecessary to use barbed wire.

ELECTRIC FENCING. If you want to divide your field at any time in order to rest your pasture during the summer months an electric fence can be useful. Obviously it cannot always be a success and in fact, where it is ideal in some circumstances it may be quite unsuitable in others. Having made use of electric fencing for some years now we have discovered through trial and error,

14

most of the advantages as well as the disadvantages. We have used it principally to divide paddocks for rotational grazing but have found it unsatisfactory for separating two groups of Donkeys. Both groups seem to lose all respect for it and somehow manage to get through, under or over it to join their friends on the other side.

We have also used two strands about 12″ to 18″ apart when mares and foals are running together as it is difficult to find a suitable height to satisfy both needs. If you use a single wire, do not have it too high as the Donkey can push under it when grazing, almost without feeling the electric shock, particularly if you have a Donkey with a thick woolly coat. We have the posts 7—10yds apart and find this distance quite satisfactory. When putting uninitiated Donkeys into a paddock with an electric fence to learn the ropes, put some wisps of hay over the wire at about 6—10ft intervals so the Donkeys can see the wire and they will then nibble the hay and discover what it is all about. Once they have been introduced to this fencing they will not forget and even after a spell without it, will remember when they meet it again and will view it with appropriate caution.

It is unwise to put a stallion in with mares he does not already know and with whom he is not familiar, because if he chases them about they will invariably go through the fence when troubled. We have used electric fencing erected about 20ft away from an ordinary fence to act as a double fence to keep a stallion away from other Donkeys. This too has been a success but the stallion had some mares running with him at the time and we cannot advise leaving a stallion on his own and separating him from other mares by an electric fence only. We found that when he was with his own mares he paced up and down for a while and then soon settled down.

Lastly, whenever electric fencing is used it is advisable to keep an eye on it frequently at first until the Donkeys are accustomed to it, and even then to check it twice a day. Although we have not had any Donkeys caught in it, there could be a first time.

STABLE. Having sorted out the fencing arrangements, some form of shelter must be your next consideration. From absolutely every point of view, particularly if you are only having one shelter, it is advantageous to have this in the Donkey's field. You will find a Donkey uses it a great deal, especially when the weather is cold and the snow is on the ground or when it is very hot and the flies are troublesome.

Stabling for a Donkey need not be too elaborate, but if you are going to put up a shed for your new Donkey it is advisable to make it large enough so that you can move around inside it with your Donkey. It is also useful to have a door or some method of shutting your Donkey inside the stable when necessary, perhaps in cases of sickness or for grooming and so on. I suggest it should be 8ft x 8ft. This may not always be possible, but as long as your Donkey has some sort of shelter in its field, too much luxury is not important. If it is in a dry corner of your field you will probably find that an earth floor is quite adequate particularly in the summer, and several different kinds of bedding can be used which I will mention in detail later.

MATERIALS FOR SHED. Interlace fencing in sections made to measure, with kicking boards nailed inside after erection, or the sides made with ordinary boarding, is quite adequate.

Asbestos sheeting for the roof, sloping from front to rear is also satisfactory and guttering can be fixed along the back so that rain water can be collected into a tank for drinking. Donkeys drink a great deal of water and it is therefore essential to have clean water available in the field at all times. Although it is not a good thing for a Donkey to drink directly after a dry feed, if water is always there he will not be tempted to take large quantities after food.

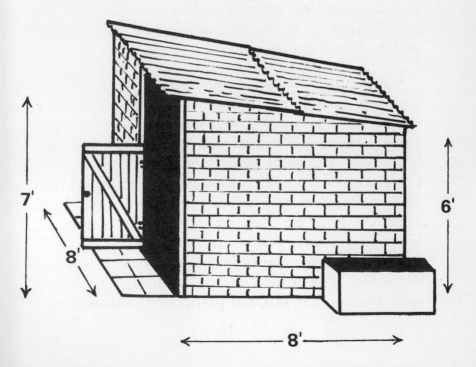

CHAPTER 3

Stable Management

FEEDING. It is advisable, as with all animals, to have a routine where feeding is concerned and to feed your Donkey at the same time each day. A little hay in summer if the grass is poor and a few pieces of carrots sliced downwards, not in rounds, apples and crusts are all very acceptable, but all things should be in moderation. Donkeys, like all equines, soon become snappy and rough if they are continually being fed tit-bits. Donkeys are just as pleased to have a visit and to be petted. Frequents visits for a little love and a pat are very valuable and such visits will also teach your Donkey to realise you come to see him at other than feeding times.

Food through the summer months, providing you have adequate grass, need really only be a token, but from about November onwards throughout the Winter it is necessary to dry feed. Hay should be given twice or even three times a day when there is snow on the ground. Give two dry feeds a day consisting of the following:-

One small handful of crushed oats, or crushed barley.
One small handful of bran and a little flaked maize.
Any additional vitamins such as Equivite Vitamin pow-

Usually donkeys enjoy feeding from the same trough

der need only be used when a mare is going to foal or if your Donkey is in very poor condition for one reason or another. Pony nuts are really too rich in protein content and tend to cause skin troubles in Donkeys, but again if your Donkey is in poor condition an odd handful of pony nuts can only do good. Donkeys are very individualistic in every way and as you get to know your Donkey you will also get to know what suits him best in the way of food.

HAY. It is important to buy good hay for Donkeys, but quite unnecessary to buy the very best or the most expensive. However, on no account should it be in any way dusty. I suggest meadow hay is the best buy. Get about half a ton at a time for one Donkey and see how far it goes. Be sure not to feed new hay cut in June until about October the same year. Because of this it is a good idea to buy your hay new when it is first cut and at its cheapest, and then store it ready for the coming winter.

A piece of rock salt placed in the stable, either in a bowl or in the manger is a great favourite as well as being good for your Donkey. This can usually be obtained from your local corn merchant.

BEDDING. As far as bedding is concerned, oat straw or wheat straw are quite suitable, but on no account allow yourself to be talked into using barley straw, as it is a great irritant to a Donkey's coat. If you have a stable with a concrete floor and luxurious draining arrangements, you will find that peat or dry wood shavings

20

can be a good form of bedding, but I cannot recommend this in an ordinary field shed as it soon becomes very soggy and messy and consequently difficult to work. However if you do put either of these types of bedding down, use plenty and have it at least 4" deep, turning it over each day after removing the droppings.

Grooming Kit. Left: a small dandy brush. Right: a dog brush (with wire teeth and wooden handle)

GROOMING. To start off your collection of grooming equipment here is a short list of a few basic necessities.
1. A Dandy Brush.
2. A Dog Brush, (with wire teeth and a wooden handle).
3. A Mane Comb, (if you have a Donkey with a long mane).
4. A Hoof Pick.
5. Two Buckets, one for water and one for food.
6. A Hay Net can be useful, but it is better to have

A wall rack is preferable to a hay net and should not be set too high

some sort of Hay Rack as Donkeys do tend to get their feet caught in a hay net and this can lead to difficulties if they are left on their own for any length of time. I only suggest a Hay Rack because if hay is just put on the ground there is so much waste.

When brushing your Donkey's head, particularly if it is young, always do it gently. In some cases a Donkey does not like having his ears touched but if you start gently handling them almost without him noticing, he will gradually get used to it. Some people have a fatal fascination for a Donkey's ears and invariably grab hold of one as soon as they are near enough, meaning it to be a friendly greeting. Children have an equal fascination for a Donkey's tail. It is advisable to educate your friends in advance into your handling and grooming methods so that they are not carried away by their enthusiasm when they come to see your new pet.

When you need to make your Donkey move his quarters from one side to the other, pushing him bodily is really quite useless; he will only push back and although you may even win in the end you are sure to be exhausted. I suggest you take the halter shank and slightly turn the Donkey's head opposite to the way you want his quarters to move, then press your hand on his quarters and tell him to move over. He will soon get the message and eventually you will only need to put your hand on his side and speak to him for him to move easily and quietly.

METHOD OF GROOMING. Use the Dandy Brush and the Dog Brush together or one at a time if used by children. Begin brushing at the head end and work back towards the tail. Brush out the knots with the Dog Brush first, using short firm strokes. Do not brush the legs too hard with this tool as the tiny wire teeth can scratch your Donkey too much when the coat is rather thin. Do not use this brush round the face for the same reason. Then in the same way brushing also the head, face and ears, use the Dandy Brush, which will bring the dust out.

You will find Donkeys usually love being brushed, especially if you start grooming from the time they are a few days old as we do. The important thing to remember is not to brush wet mud into their skin, as this can cause trouble. Always brush the hairs the same way as the coat lies. It is a good plan to brush your Donkey under his saddle after riding to make him more comfortable. Never leave him unbrushed for weeks on end because apart from the obvious discomfort this will cause, he likes being brushed and it is good to encourage him to come to you for grooming as well as for feeding.

When brushing your Donkey's tail, try not to pull it about too much. Use a Dog Brush first and then brush it to strand it nicely. This is usually better than using a mane comb which has rather widely spaced teeth.

FEET. Picking your Donkey's feet up is all part of his education and I suggest that you pick them up as part of your grooming routine so that when the farrier does come your Donkey has a general idea of what is required of him. You should stand with your back towards the Donkey's head, close into his body, run the hand nearest to the Donkey down its leg from the top to the hoof and leaning slightly against him invite him to pick his foot up. As at all times talk to him and make all your movements firm and definite.

BLACKSMITH AND CARE OF FEET. The next thing to consider are your Donkey's hooves which should be pared back by your Blacksmith at least once every three months. It

24

is quite unnecessary to put shoes on a Donkey's feet. Although it is a good thing to keep your Donkey's feet cleaned out, do not be too enthusiastic with your hoof pick, particularly round the frog, which is the soft triangular piece at the centre back of the sole of the hoof, or with a young Donkey whose hooves are not properly formed and are still growing, as you might do much more harm than good. Hoof oil painted on the hooves every now and then is both good for the hoof and looks very smart particularly if you are showing your Donkey.

Eating hay from a circular wire hay rack

CHAPTER 4

Ailments

ILLNESS. I suggest you invest in a small veterinary box consisting of the following items which you can obtain either from your veterinary surgeon or your Chemist.
1. Worm Powders. There are four types of worms to be dealt with in Donkeys. a) Redworms or Strongyles. b) Roundworms. c) Ascarid worms. d) Lung worm.

Owing to recent research there are now several effective products on the market, and I suggest you consult your Vet about this. He will advise you on which he considers is the most satisfactory. If a powder form is used it can be mixed in with a dry feed or dissolved in water and then added to the feed. It is a good idea to keep a note of the dates of worming in your diary for future reference after each dose is given.
2. A medicated animal shampoo is also a good standby in cases of many skin troubles or scurviness of any sort. Rub it on to the affected areas and leave for some minutes before rinsing. It is important to rinse very thoroughly before drying with a rough towel.
3. A small bottle of antiseptic powder is useful in case your Donkey scratches or cuts itself.

4. A bottle of antiseptic is always necessary. Only weak solutions of antiseptic should be used. Often a salt solution is preferable for bathing wounds.

5. Cotton Wool.

6. Louse Powder.

These are just a few bits and pieces which you will find are in constant use. Later on you may wish to become more ambitious and have your own thermometer and other items, but I do feel that it is essential to use these only after discussion with your Vet and after you have gradually gained practical experience.

It is wise to have your Donkey inoculated against Tetanus.

COLIC. Your Donkey can get colic for a number of reasons. Drinking a lot of water after food or when very hot. Eating new hay or wet bread and many other things could result in stomach pains. Incidentally do remind your neighbours not to feed your pet on meat sandwiches. The symptoms of colic are normally those of abdominal pain. This can be due to several causes, some more serious than others. If your Donkey seems restless and lies down and continually wants to roll and is not himself, you can generally assume the reason is colic. Call in your Vet and until your help comes along try to stop the animal rolling. Either walk him up and down or at least keep him on his feet. He can damage himself internally if he rolls about. The pain may clear itself but unless you have experience in drenching it is not advisable to attempt to give your Donkey a Colic drink until your Vet arrives.

LAMINITIS. This is an inflammation in the feet and is usually caused by too rich grass or over eating. It causes the Donkey a great deal of discomfort and he tends to want to lie down and appears to be lame on the forelegs or occasionally all legs. With luck and good judgement you may catch laminitis in the early stages. As it usually comes with the Spring grass which is young and rich, he must be taken off the grass at once. In a bad case he must be kept in his stable. A little hay and water is all he must eat for a day or two until there are signs of improvement. As the effects of severe laminitis can result in permanent lameness it is essential to call in your Vet as soon as possible. The Donkey should not be ridden during this time, but when the worst is over short walks on a leading rein can only be beneficial.

RINGWORM. This is a very infectious skin disease, but I do think Donkeys like other animals tend to build up a natural immunity. It is a beastly skin complaint and appears in round hard scabby patches, but diagnosis on appearance alone is not always easy. The scabs should be removed by hand when they start to dry underneath and then painted as recommended by your Vet with a suitable preparation. Widespread infection can be treated with a drug given by mouth. Ringworm can be very unsightly, but if treated early and regularly it should soon clear up and new hair will start to grow where the patches have been. Ringworm is infectious to human beings.

BOG ITCH. This is caused by constant dampness on the legs and feet and the hair on the Donkey's legs falls out lea-

A medicine cupboard

ving bald patches. It is more prevalent in young Donkeys. It is by no means infectious or contagious and
can be rubbed with vaseline or in bad cases, a proprie-
tory ointment can be obtained from your Vet, who will
advise you on this point.

SCOURING. There are a number of reasons why a Donkey
scours. Too much grass, frosted grass, too damp bran
mash, or an infection. If it continues beyond a day or
two, and after keeping an eye on your Donkey's diet,

you must call your Vet. Scouring in young foals may result from a change in the mother's milk which often occurs when she comes into season. It may however result from infection. This is serious and should receive immediate attention. You will find as you become familiar with your Donkey that you will soon know when remedial measures have to be taken.

COUGHS AND COLDS. Coughs and running noses can result in something more serious. More serious virus of the flu type will cause the animal to run a temperature in addition to the other signs, which will show itself in a listless and dejected Donkey. In all cases consult your Vet. A Donkey very quickly gets a secondary infection. I cannot stress too forcefully the importance of dealing with these colds and coughs at once and if you do, you may avoid a great deal of worry and trouble.

LUNG WORM.   Coughing in Donkeys is frequently associated with the presence of lungworms. The subject is a complex one, and further research is needed.

The parasite responsible for the disease in the Donkey can also infest horses and ponies. It does appear, however, that the Donkey is more easily infected than the horse, and at the same time is more able to tolerate an infestation. Infection may be passed from Donkeys to other equines, but the risk to horses will vary with circumstances. Advice should be sought before mixing the two species.

Immature worms (or larvae) are passed to the pasture in the dung of an infected animal. After a period of time, these larvae become infective, and when eaten,

A light-weight blanket-rug tied with tape round the chest and surcingle also tied with tapes on top of back can be useful when a Donkey has a cold

pass through the body, returning to the lungs where the life cycle is completed.

As with most diseases, infection eventually results in the development of an immunity. Thus it is young animals and those that have not previously been exposed to infection that are most susceptible.

Immunity is not complete, and animals may harbour small numbers of worms in their lungs for many years and continue to infect the pasture.

Diagnosis of the disease by examining the dung for the presence of lungworm larvae is commonly practised; the assumption being that their absence is evidence of freedom from disease. This is not necessarily true, as in some cases, worms may be present in the lungs, but, because of partial immunity, fail to produce larvae, either

31

permanently or for a period of time. It is thus possible that the apparently disease-free animal may, at a later date, again commence excreting larvae in the dung and infecting the pasture.

From the foregoing it will be seen that it is wise to regard all Donkeys as infected with lungworm, and to practice routine worming. Worming will not only reduce the level of infestation of the individual, but will keep the pasture level of infection as low as possible. Short term rotation of pastures returning to the same grazing after only a few weeks rest, is, in itself, of little value in the control of the disease. Pasture found to be infected should be rested for at least twelve months.

In heavy infestations the lung damage produced may result in secondary bacterial pneumonias, and virus infections of the lungs may be more serious in the presence of lungworms. Provided that adequate control measures are practiced, 'lungworm' in itself need not be a cause for major worry.

Even if you only have one Donkey it is advisable to keep a record of medical treatment, worming, seasons if you have a mare, and farrier. If you have more than one Donkey it is essential to keep records.

INSURANCE. Most Insurance Brokers will offer you cover for your Donkey. I think it is well worthwhile taking this up because the annual premium is very small in comparison to the loss of your Donkey. You will be asked to supply a Veterinary Certificate confirming that your Donkey is fit at the time you take out the Insurance and thereafter annually at the time of renewal.

CHAPTER 5

Training and Riding

If your Donkey once begins to kick or bite seriously, this is not always easy to put right. I feel it is most important, particularly if you have a young Donkey, never to allow these situations to arise. Prevention is very much better than cure, which in any case may never be complete.

When walking round the back of your Donkey rest your hand firmly on him so that he knows you are there and that you are not doing anything sinister. Once again talk to him. I am quite sure that once a young Donkey becomes familiar with all you are doing and that all situations which may cause him to develop bad habits are avoided by careful handling, such ideas will not come into his head. The same applies to bad habits when being ridden. If a child is allowed to throw itself onto a Donkey, race it round and round a field or jump it over the same jump until it is bored to death, even a Donkey will retaliate. The trouble in the past has been that Donkeys were not trained quietly with understanding and respect, and in consequence they have a reputation for bucking and being stubborn. I am quite sure that if a Donkey behaves like this there will be a past history of advantage being taken of its long suffering nature. People should not abuse their good fortune in having such a tolerant pet. To gain your Donkey's respect means that you have to achieve quite a high standard of behaviour yourself.

HARNESS. If you have added a six-month-old foal to your family it will not be necessary to consider harness immediately, as a Donkey should be at least 18 months old before any weight is put on his back. As far as real riding is concerned it is advisable to wait until your Donkey is two years old. However when the time does come, a bridle with an ordinary broken snaffle bit and a Numnah Pad Saddle with stirrups and leathers is all that is really necessary for a beginner. Until this stage is reached a halter should be in constant use particularly with a young Donkey. The more often the halter is put on and the Donkey led about the easier it will be when you really want to take your Donkey out for a walk or start to ride him. If and when the time comes that you want to show your Donkey, it will be necessary to invest in a leather headcollar unless you show him in his saddle and bridle in a riding class. I use three sizes of Donkey halters which are made from canvas webbing with a rope shank, which I find extremely useful especially when the Donkeys are growing and move up from one size to another.

Although Donkeys are very placid by nature it is always possible to spoil them as it is any animal. And when a Donkey is young, as with all young things, a certain amount of discipline is essential. Children always tend to want to run towards an animal and it is

A Donkey saddled and bridled

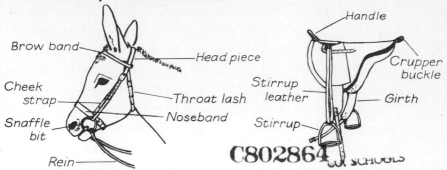

Brow band — Head piece

Cheek strap — Throat lash

Snaffle bit — Noseband

Rein — Handle

Stirrup leather — Crupper buckle

Stirrup — Girth

C802864 SCHOOLS

Snaffle bridle with noseband. Noseband can be worn but is not always necessary.

Numnah saddle without crupper. The crupper is used to prevent the saddle slipping forward and has a loop for the tail to go through.

Top: Eggbutt jointed snaffle bit
Below: Half moon nylon snaffle bit

as well to teach them to walk towards their new pet, and when approaching him, to put their hand under his chin to stroke him. This is to avoid the possibility of him moving away at the sight of a large hand coming over the front of his face. Once you have gained his confidence he will soon accept your hand of friendship, and can then of course be stroked wherever you like. In the early stages it is important to teach children to treat the rear end of their Donkey with respect and not to hang on to his tail or always be patting his rump. Donkeys should not kick if they are handled well from the beginning but for future years when children move on to the pony stage it is well to start with good habits. Some Donkeys like their ears stroked, some do not, but they will soon let you know their individual likes and dislikes.

When putting on a halter everything should be done from the side as far as possible. The 'near side' is the

A canvas halter

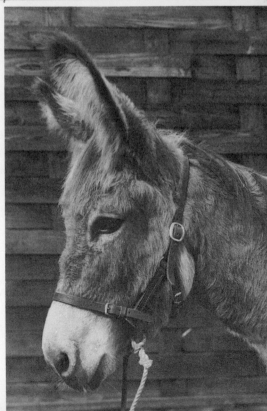

A correctly fitting head collar

left-hand side of the Donkey and the 'off side' is the right-hand side. All these manoeuvres should be carried out from the near side, and this is a moment when a tit-bit is thoroughly recommended. Go up to your Donkey with a tit-bit in your hand, give it to him, move round to the near side and put your hand on his shoulder, sliding the rope shank of the halter over his neck so that you can hold him firmly while putting the halter over his head and getting it into the correct position. He will not then be able to move away and you will not have several false starts. I think this system is advisable even with older Donkeys. I do feel that a few tips of this kind can make life much easier for both Donkey and owner.

Now you are ready to start and lead him forwards. Always remember that if he is reluctant to move no amount of pulling is going to make your Donkey move forward and pushing does not help a great deal either. Apart from the other obvious reasons against these methods they can be extremely exhausting. In fact to teach your Donkey to move forward it is an excellent plan to have a member of the family walking just behind with another leading the Donkey on the near side. A small switch not less than 3ft long can be held in the leader's left hand so that it can be used without turning right round. This, together with the helper at the rear, if necessary putting a hand on the Donkey's rump to let him know someone is there, should produce the desired effect and make your Donkey move forward when the correct command of 'walk' is given. Sometimes if a young Donkey insists on moving his quarters away from you to avoid the switch, a rope attached to his halter on the off side, brought loosely round his hind quarters and held by the leader will help. Naturally it is easier to be without too many trappings. Use your switch carefully and never over use it. Teach your Donkey not to be afraid of it, just to respect it. Be careful not to wave it around his face even by accident. Although this may all sound a little complicated, when put into practice there should be no problems and soon the switch may be forgotten and the Donkey will move forward because he understands what you want him to do. Donkeys, although determined personalities, are always anxious to please. The important thing to remember is to make quite sure that you have put your message over to him correctly before condemning him. A few definite and simple consistent words of command such as 'walk', 'trot', 'halt' and so on all help to produce a willing and obedient Donkey.

RIDING. When you have a young Donkey about two years old and ready to be taught to carry passengers, start by fitting his bridle. As mentioned earlier use an ordinary snaffle bit. It is quite unnecessary to use a mouthing bit with Donkeys as you do with horses although some people do.

BRIDLING. First put the reins over the Donkey's head, hold the top of the bridle in your right hand and put your left hand under the bit. Holding the bridle over his face put your left thumb gently in the corner of the Donkey's mouth, where there are no teeth of course.

He will then open his mouth and you can then slip the bit in and carefully pull the headpiece of the bridle over your Donkey's ears. Take a look to see everything has landed in the right place, be sure that the bit is not too tight by seeing that the corners of the mouth are only just creased, then finally secure throat lash and noseband. The Donkey will feel his bit with his tongue and play with it for a short while, but will soon get used to the new sensation. I think it is a good idea to leave the bit in the Donkey's mouth and lead him around a little for two or three days, to get him used to the whole idea before putting on the saddle.

SADDLING UP. The next step is to fit his saddle. Place this up above his withers on his mane and slide it down onto his back. The front of the saddle should be just below the withers. Put your hand on top of the saddle and press it down so that he understands what you are doing then pull the girth through and do it up lightly at first. When the girth is finally tightened you should be able to slide four fingers of your left hand under it. Do not do it up so tightly that your Donkey is uncomfortable. Once again it is advisable to give this a trial run for a day or two before mounting. When using a pad saddle I suggest having a crupper which the tail should be put through making sure the hairs at the top are not caught in any way. The strap of the crupper is then put through the loop at the back of the saddle and fastened, not too tightly. You should be able to put four fingers upright under the centre of the strap. If you are an old hand at backing Donkeys and Horses you will know when the right moment for mounting comes along, but if it is something you have never done before, or seen anyone else do, it is always wise to be a little cautious although you will probably find your Donkey will accept everything as a matter of course.

MOUNTING. Now your Donkey is ready to be mounted. The child must take the reins in the left hand also holding the front of the saddle with the same hand. Put the left foot in the stirrup and swing the right leg over the saddle putting the right foot into the other stirrup . Make sure all is in place, hold a rein in each hand, have someone leading to start with and you are now ready to give your Donkey his first lesson in elementary aids.

ELEMENTARY AIDS. These are the recognised methods of communication between you and your Donkey. To move forward, slightly loosen your reins, lean forward a little and squeeze with your legs. Try to avoid too much flapping about with your legs; it looks so untidy and I believe this causes the animal to become confused and unsure about the whole message. To halt, pull gently on the reins and squeeze slightly with the legs.

To turn to the right shorten the right rein, lay the left rein on the near side of the neck and squeeze with the right leg. To turn to the left do exactly the reverse. Be patient and persevere, the results can be very rewarding. Take it gently at first. A short walk around for the first day or two is all that should be expected. Gradually each day after this you can become more ambitious. Do not let your Donkey become bored by walking him round and round in a dull circle, take him somewhere different and vary your lesson so that you keep his interest as well as your own.

DISMOUNTING. When the time comes to dismount, take both feet out of the stirrups and still holding the reins in the left hand swing the right leg over the Donkey's hindquarters and so on to the ground. Do not let go of the reins even then. Slip both reins over the Donkey's head holding them together in your right hand, lead your Donkey into its stable to have the harness removed, or if in the field loop your reins over your left arm to secure your Donkey so that he cannot move off without you knowing about it. Slide the stirrups up to the top of the leathers so that they do not dangle about and tuck the leathers through the stirrup irons. Then undo the girth, placing it over the top of the saddle and so lift the saddle off. Undo the throat lash and noseband on the bridle. If you are going to replace it with a halter, slip the halter shank round the Donkey's neck before removing the bridle, so that he will not walk away. The most important part of all this is to avoid doing anything with fuss and noise. I do believe that one's whole behaviour with any animal has a lasting and important bearing on its attitude to everything. Particularly with young Donkeys, if you are fussed and bothered and dart about in a great state, you transmit your mood straight to the animal, if not at once, certainly in the long run and this takes time and hard work to undo. I think children must be taught to respect their new pet and in fact must learn to do all the little chores connected with the Donkey as far as possible, and so grow up to realise that stable management is 90% of the pleasure of riding Donkeys and perhaps later on ponies and horses. It certainly pays parents to insist on their children doing all these things themselves and it proves of great benefit later on when the children can be their own grooms!

TRAINING

If you do not know exactly what to do it is easy to have setbacks when training your Donkey. Even when he becomes an old hand at all the arts of life it is as well to continue with your methods and these should in time become perfectly natural to you both.

Even a simple exercise such as leading a Donkey through a gateway or into his stable can be a hazardous adventure if you are not careful. Leading on the near side move to the front of him and look back just to make sure the gap is wide enough. Have your gate or door open properly. If you have been out riding and your Donkey is still saddled and bridled, before you take him into the stable make sure that the stirrups are either crossed or slid up to the top of the leathers and tucked through the irons so that there is nothing dangling around. Also slip the reins over his head so that if he pulls away from you for any unforseen reason, you have a longer rein to hold on to. This also avoids the possibility of the rein being caught on anything as you go through the door.

If you are going to leave your Donkey alone for a few minutes in the stable before unsaddling, make sure the reins are either knotted in riding position or one side tucked under a stirrup. All sorts of trouble can be caused if he gets his feet in his own rein or if they catch anything when no one is about.

I would also suggest loosening the girth a little as this may prove to be very uncomfortable to the Donkey after being ridden.

I must add that even after all this you should not leave your Donkey waiting for more than a few minutes after a ride. As soon as possible his saddle and bridle should be taken off and the hairs under the saddle either brushed to make him comfortable, or if wet, rubbed with a wisp made of hay or straw. You can quickly make this by twisting some lengths of hay or straw together into a circular pad. With this sort of wisp there is no risk of rubbing the damp into the skin.

We have our Donkeys near the house and in the summer as well as sometimes in the winter they are invited to come into the house. Once young ones have taken the step and ventured through the door you will find they usually settle down all too well. We frequently find we have to resort to a tit-bit to persuade them to return to their friends. A small word of warning, if you do have your pet in the house from time to time, he will be very interested in the floral decorations and it is as well to put these out of reach! We always find that Donkeys are naturally clean in the house, at least for an hour or two.

Donkeys are generally very clean animals with ordered habits. So far we have never had an accident in the house but I expect there will be a first time one day.

One of our Donkeys who became a frequent visitor to the drawing-room when she was not too well, used to come into the house looking for me. If she could not find me in the drawing-room she would wend her way out again, along passages and down steps without fear of doing damage, on her way to another haunt of mine where she thought I might be found. She was about the most intelligent Donkey I have ever come across. She used to rest her head on my shoulder while I was writing letters at my desk and if she thought it was time we did something more interesting she would go to the nearest vase of flowers and stand beside it. She knew she must not touch the flowers but would threaten me with that possibility. Nothing seems to startle Donkeys inside the house any more than outside. I always find they make sure of the floor covering on their first visit; fitted carpets are preferred!

Haywisps for drying
your donkey

CHAPTER 6

Showing

SHOWING. If you are thinking of showing your little Donkey I would suggest you join the Donkey Breed Society. The Society is affiliated to the British Horse Society and even if you do not show I am sure you would find their magazines with so many helpful hints and with other Donkey owners' experiences, most valuable. There are several different Donkey Classes at most of the Agricultural Shows and Horse Shows now and there are some shows entirely for Donkeys. The most important thing before getting your application form from the Show Secretary is to make sure you have time before the show to teach your Donkey the form so that he will be quite familiar with Show routine when the time comes. At the moment if you are showing in hand (leading), or riding, your Donkey will be expected to walk round the Show ring with all the other Donkeys in the Class, holding his head up and walking out well, until the Judge selects those he wishes to come out and stand in line side by side, so that he can look at them more carefully later on. If you are lucky enough to be called second or third or wherever it is, walk to the near side of the last Donkey to form the line down the centre of the ring and stand in front of your Donkey. When he is ready the Judge will start to look at each Donkey in the line individually. You will be asked to lead your Donkey out in front of the others and walk him away from the Judge in a straight line and then turn him and trot him back towards the Judge, then return to your place in line. Always lead on the near side and when turning your Donkey always turn him away from you, so following his head round. It is a good idea to go over the routine with your Donkey each day for several days before the Show giving him quiet and definite words of command and encouragement.

BOXING. If you have your own transport this is of course the best arrangement, since time is all yours and there is no need to be in any hurry when teaching your Donkey to enter the trailer or horse box. You must be patient when you give him his first lesson as it is all very strange to him to be confronted with an odd looking box at the top of a slope on wheels, which wobbles a bit into the bargain. You may find you have several false starts but never despair. If he is very young and travelling with his mother he can be carried into the box to start with. Put your arms round the front of his chest and under the back of his legs and so pick him up firmly. As soon as possible teach him to take the plunge himself as this is so much easier for all concerned. A small door in the front of the box is useful and I think if someone stands outside this open door holding a bowl of food this will help. With a little family assistance behind, with someone leading the Donkey also with a

bowl of tit-bits he may well go up the ramp without too much trouble. You can give him a little help if he is hesitant and place one of his forefeet on the ramp when this is possible. Do not pull, he will only get frightened, and this is not promising for the next time you have to go through the performance. He can be held firmly but do not fight with him. Hold the bowl of food low down on the ramp so that he can see both the food and what his feet are doing at the same time.

If the matter becomes too difficult and he simply will not be persuaded, link arms with another helper

and with the leader still at the front, place your linked arms under and round the Donkey's hindquarters. This has proved a great success and we have found that it does not need too much strength even with awkward customers. Once he is in and his feet are off the ramp, quickly raise the ramp to stop him coming out. The person at the door in the front can then distract your Donkey with the tit-bits. The important thing about dealing with animals is to be ready and anticipate, just in case you need to be resourceful. I do believe it is important to talk to your Donkey. They always seem to find a quiet soft voice reassuring and this should be used as often as possible. When harnessing him or grooming or even feeding, tell him what you are doing while you do it. He may not understand exactly what you are saying, but from your tone of voice indicating that all is well you gain his confidence and he learns to trust you.

Donkeys usually travel very well and enjoy looking at the view, unlike a horse or pony who would be terrified at the sight of traffic passing by. Our Donkeys always seem to stand by the window in our box just in case they miss anything.

Donkeys are very sensible about traffic too, and if they are introduced to it in small doses from the time they are young foals they will accept it all as just part of life. They are extremely intelligent animals and they seem to find it easy to overcome any fears once they understand what is going on.

Oliver, our labrador, with his two playmates

RELATIONSHIPS WITH DOGS. It might be helpful to dog owners to mention a few points about relationships between dogs and Donkeys. Donkeys do not seem to take to dogs at once and some can even be aggressive. Much depends on the temperament of both dog and Donkey. Certainly if they are introduced quietly and gradually they learn to accept each other and become great friends. Some Donkeys are indifferent to dogs but if they are bothered by them it is well to persuade your friends to keep their strange dogs out of the field, particularly if you have a mare with a foal at foot, as she does not really like even other Donkeys to pay too much attention to her new baby never mind dogs. Donkeys usually become great friends with the dogs in the family where they are living, once they have both decided that they have equal rights to be there and have become familiar with each other's idiosyncrasies and arrive at a mutual understanding.

CHAPTER 7

Breeding

FOALING. If you have a little mare and one day you feel that it would be fun to put her into foal, there are several points to be considered. A Donkey mare usually starts to come into season sometime during her second spring or summer and you can have her served at this time and she will then have her first foal as a three year old. It takes any time between eleven and thirteen months to produce a foal but usually it is over twelve months. Donkey mares come into season every three weeks and when you have selected a suitable stallion, make sure he has a nice temperament as well as good conformation. I suggest that if this is to be the mare's first foal she should be either left with the stallion over two seasons, or make two visits. Seasons, as I have already said, come every three weeks through the summer months but usually stop through the winter months. Spring or early summer is the best time to take your mare to stud. We have found that it is advisable to rest a very young mare after her first foal, but failing this she may automatically not come into season again during the summer her foal is at foot and so gives herself a rest. She will however probably start to come into season again very early the following year in January or February and in consequence may have a winter foal the next year. It is important to keep the foal dry for at least three months in spite of its nice woolly coat and if the weather is bad you do need to keep an eye on this. Even in the middle of summer whenever it is raining hard it is wise to bring the foal inside with its mother until it is at least three months old.

A Donkey usually attends to the whole matter of having her foal all by herself. On no account try to help her even if you feel worried. Unless you are really experienced it is much better to call your Vet. Too little knowledge can be an extremely dangerous thing at these times. Although she will enjoy your visits and words of encouragement you will be lucky if you see your foal arriving. Donkeys do like to do these things in private, and I think it is a good thing to let them carry on alone as far as possible providing all is obviously going well. In other words do not sit up all night as well as all day and watch her. It may worry her and will certainly worry you.

We always begin to get anxious at about eleven months and look each day to see if there is any change. About a month before the foal arrives she will start bagging up, this means she is beginning to have milk ready for the foal, although sometimes with a first foal this bagging up may be very slight before foaling, but invariably within twenty-four hours of foaling she will have an ample supply of milk. When small drops of wax appear on the teats you may be sure that within ten days or so your foal will be born. Just before she is due to foal the lower part of the spine becomes soft and flexible in preparation for the arrival and then, one morning, all being well your new foal will be there to greet you. Everyone can then heave a sigh of relief as the strain will have been enormous.

I hope everything will be as you anticipate and that the new addition to your family will be strong, well, and that everything will be straightforward.

The whole birth usually takes about 30–40 minutes, each stage being very rapid. If you do see the arrival and once all is obviously well, leave the mare to clean up her baby and while she is doing this the afterbirth should come away. This should be removed and buried.

It will be a great temptation to go straight up to the foal, but it is wise to restrain yourself. Go first to the mare, make a big fuss of her and tell her how clever she has been before addressing yourself to her new off-spring. I cannot help feeling this is just Donkey psychology! Anyway it certainly ensures that she will allow you to handle her foal and attend to the necessary without fuss or worry. You will find if she is with other Donkeys they will not be allowed to speak to the foal for a day or so, only admire it from a discreet distance. It is important to give the mare a bran mash and while she is eating this you can quietly dress the foal's navel. This is essential to prevent possible infection. Pick the little foal up in your arms and gently turn it over on the ground holding both front and hind legs together. If you have a helper it is then quite easy for them to paint the navel with plenty of iodine. A soft paint brush is normally used for this purpose. I usually find the foal will lie quite still and enjoy the whole thing if treated gently and have often attended to the whole matter myself without help. After this leave both mother and foal quietly alone to recover and get to know each other.

It is no use pretending that things always go well during foaling and while I do not want to put anyone off breeding their own Donkey, there are one or two possible hazards I cannot leave unmentioned, so that you can at least be prepared and may be able to do something to help. So many things can happen in practice and these never seem to be on paper.

A mother usually accepts her foal immediately, but if she does not this may be due to one of the following reasons. The foal could be weak or not quite what the mare feels is perfect. Nature then tells her to ignore the whole thing and disown her foal. This may seem hard, but it does happen. Or it can be that she just does not like the sensation of her foal sucking, or it may be that she is sensitive, perhaps she may have mastitis or some other udder infection. However, after calling your Vet you can meantime try one or two things yourself. If you think the foal appears to be quite normal and that the mare has plenty of milk, it is worth trying for a while to hold the little foal up in your arms and try to persuade it to take the milk from its mother itself. If the mare is very tiresome, a helper at each end of the Donkey is really necessary, but if two people are not available have one person holding a rope round the mother's hind leg to try to stop her kicking while you hold up the foal. You will, of course, have to tie the mother's head and distract her with food, preferably her favourite dish whatever it is! I have tried this quite sucessfully even though it was rather hard work. However if it comes off you avoid all the business of bottle feeding afterwards. If you persist with this effort without being kicked across the box too many times it is certainly worthwhile and it works. If it is merely the new sensation caused by the foal feeding which the mare takes exception to she will soon become accustomed to it. This does not only necessarily happen with a first foal. In fact Donkeys are their usual unpredictable selves at all times including foaling.

If you do not have fairly rapid results with this method do not wait too long before milking the mother and feeding the milk from a baby's bottle, which you should include in your Veterinary Box before you start breeding your own Donkeys. Use large teats, preferably the sort used for calves. The important thing is not to let the little foal become too weak before bottle feeding. Teach it to suck by putting your fingers in its mouth; it will soon get the message. The mother's milk during the first 48 hours after foaling is invaluable to the foal. Sometimes salt sprinkled on the baby's coat will persuade the mother to accept her foal but it is worth trying anything and everything you can think of while waiting for your Vet to arrive. It is wise to let him check your new foal in any case, and after 24 hours he can then issue a health certificate and you can make arrangements to include it on your Insurance Policy.

The National Foaling Bank offers a useful service in cases where foals are without mothers and vice versa, and if you are desperate it would be as well to see if they can help.

The other point is that the mare may not have enough milk and you will have to supplement with 4 - 6 oz of cow's milk in a baby's bottle every four hours for a few days until the mother gradually produces enough herself. However it is advisable to consult your Vet about this.

FRIENDSHIPS AND RELATIONSHIPS WITH PEOPLE AND EACH OTHER

People find it difficult to understand how anyone can ever differentiate between their Donkeys but I can never quite understand the reasoning behind this. After all, most people know the difference between dogs of the same breed. However, to turn to the other side of the picture, a Donkey certainly knows the difference between people. They love people with whom they can make lasting friendships just as they do among themselves. Most of ours have their own special friend. At one time we were left with one odd Donkey after the others had all paired off, so we bought another. Our new one was a very independent little person and really was not interested in either finding a friend or in fact meeting other Donkeys. She was eighteen months old, had never seen another Donkey since she left her mother's apron strings and we were quite sure she thought she was a human being. However, our lone Donkey just followed her about everywhere wearing a look which said 'you are going to be my friend whether you like it or not'. Eventually they met half way and a splendid friendship developed. Both have very strong characters and they now have fierce disagreements but I know that they understand each other and do not like to be parted for too long. At times when they are both having their foals they become slightly independent again, but when the summer has passed and their babies have grown up, once again they become inseparable companions.

Each Donkey has its own special personality and each is a complete individual. They have traits which appear from birth and I believe that many characteristics, even behaviour, are hereditary. We have had numerous foals who were exactly like their mothers both in looks, personality and attitude to life. One was the daughter of a shy mother and needed just the same reassurance as her mother had needed before her. It is very important to spend time on such a foal so that she will grow to have more confidence in human beings. You can certainly lessen the shyness even though you may never be able to eradicate it completely. If this type of Donkey is ever harshly treated, within seconds all your hard work can be undone. She will only respond well to kindness and understanding. Equally, if you have a rather bouncing, confident foal, for its own sake it may well have to be corrected from time to time, firmly, kindly, but never with a stick as the tone of voice is much more effective with all animals particularly Donkeys, whom I consider have a very high I.Q. Praise your Donkey whenever possible so that when you do have to reprimand him he knows you mean business.

TALKING POINTS. Each Donkey has a different voice, all

its own and although some can be noisy, there may well be a reason for this. It can be that a mare is in season, or lonely, but usually, although striking a rather sad sounding note, they are just greeting you or reminding you it is feed time. We find our Donkeys very often just quietly talk to us while we are busying about the place. We have long ago forgotten what it is like not to hear their music from time to time.

We have a Donkey mare who sings for her supper. She shuts her eyes and you can see her listening to herself. We have only ever had one who did this and did not believe we could ever have another until this year when she foaled. Now at four months old her little daughter joins in and they make the most wonderful music together as the little one seems to have a slightly deeper voice, which harmonises perfectly with mum's falsetto. These two are identical personalities and they even look alike. Father does not seem to have taken any part in her make-up.

If you have a stallion running with your mare or mares it is best to leave them together when the foal is due so that he is around when it is born and will accept it. Sometimes if you put a mother with a new foal which is unknown to your stallion, back into the herd the stallion may attack it. I think even if you have more than one mare it is best to leave them all together too. We find that the other mares usually take on the rather special duty of Aunty.

We never leave our mares, which are due to foal, with a horse or pony. It is advisable to separate mare and foal from horses and ponies for a period of six months or so, and to allow contact over the fence only, so that they become familiar with each other before the foal is weaned and old enough to stand up for itself a little.

Horses and ponies have such completely different temperaments to Donkeys and must be introduced over a fence when young, Donkeys just do not understand too much squealing and kicking however friendly it may be. Horses and Donkeys usually become excellent companions and the only problem can be that they may become inseparable.

WEANING. Mother and foal must remain together for at least six months, then the foal should be weaned. It begins to place a heavy burden on the mare if they are left together too long particularly if the mare is in foal again. We feel that a mare should be served during her second season after foaling, so six months is quite long enough for her to be feeding her foal at foot. Ideally when weaning, the foal is best out of sight of its mother. Separate them perhaps while the mare is feeding and has her mind on other things. When six months have gone by the mare is already a little indifferent to her foal and if you are lucky she just accepts that it has gone. We have been quite successful with most of ours but here as each one pairs up with another little friend things are bound to be easier. We try to arrange to wean ours in pairs and this has proved to be very satisfactory. After a month or so you will find you can put your Donkey foal with its mother again and they will then be just good friends.

CHAPTER 8

Driving

If you do ever decide to harness your Donkey to a trap in order to drive, you will have to enlist the help of several members of the family to begin with. But first there is the problem of finding a governess cart or small pony trap, which may take some time, as also will a set of harness. You will find people offer you all kinds of rubbish before you finally find what you think is right for your Donkey. What we call the working harness, which has a heavy type of collar, can be used, but I think the American type which has a leather strap type collar is used more often nowadays. Once you have acquired a set of harness, which incidentally is not a cheap item, get your Donkey thoroughly used to having it put on and taken off, and most of all let him become used to the odd jangling noises. Do this for several days, leading him about with it on so that he becomes really accustomed to it. You may find that the Donkey will feel it is all rather strange at first so take it slowly. If you cannot manage to fit it yourself it is wise to find a friend who can give you a hand. Then with someone at the head holding the bridle and you at the rear holding the long reins, you are ready to move forwards, but without the trap for the first few days. Driving from behind, you will find that gradually the leader becomes less operative, eventually just walking alongside. All instructions must come from the driver.

By the time you come to putting your Donkey into his trap he should be quite used to all the strange noises and routine of the harness, and if he is now simply led for a while when in the trap the driver will soon be able to take over. Talk constantly to your Donkey. Voice is terribly important. A whip is essential but be careful not to irritate your Donkey with it. I think driving is something you can learn a great deal about as you go along. Experience is certainly a great help but if you have no experience try to keep a day or two ahead of your Donkey in lessons.

*   *   *

Finally if you have read all of this you may feel that owning a Donkey is not for you. If this is so then it is much better that you have found out before taking a Donkey into your family circle. But if, in spite of what you have read, you still feel Donkeys are a 'must' in your family, then I know that the whole adventure will give you and your family the greatest of pleasure and that the relationship between you and your new pet can only be successful and happy.

Useful Addresses

Donkey Breed Society,
Hon. Secretary,
Mrs. Walter Greenway,
Prouts Farm,
Hawkley,
Nr. Liss,
Hampshire.

The American Donkey and Mule Society,
Secretary-Editor
Mule Registrar,
Mrs. Betsy Hutchins,
Route 1,
Box 519.A,
Denton,
Texas,
76201, U.S.A.

The National Foaling Bank,
Miss Johanna Vardon,
Meretown Stud,
Newport,
Shropshire.

The Irish Donkey Society,
Hon. Secretary,
35 Cecil Street,
Limerick.